A CHANGE IN
Perception

DIVINELY INSPIRED BY SOMETHING GREATER
THAN MYSELF, THAT CONNECTS US ALL

Sherryl Comeau

BALBOA.PRESS

A DIVISION OF HAY HOUSE

Balboa Press books may be ordered through booksellers or by contacting:

Balboa Press
A Division of Hay House
1663 Liberty Drive
Bloomington, IN 47403
www.balboapress.com
1 (877) 407-4847

Because of the dynamic nature of the Internet, any web addresses or links contained in this book may have changed since publication and may no longer be valid. The views expressed in this work are solely those of the author and do not necessarily reflect the views of the publisher, and the publisher hereby disclaims any responsibility for them.

The author of this book does not dispense medical advice or prescribe the use of any technique as a form of treatment for physical, emotional, or medical problems without the advice of a physician, either directly or indirectly. The intent of the author is only to offer information of a general nature to help you in your quest for emotional and spiritual well-being. In the event you use any of the information in this book for yourself, which is your constitutional right, the author and the publisher assume no responsibility for your actions.

Print information available on the last page.

ISBN: 978-1-9822-4034-9 (sc)
ISBN: 978-1-9822-4035-6 (hc)
ISBN: 978-1-9822-4036-3 (e)

Library of Congress Control Number: 2019920822

Balboa Press rev. date: 12/23/2019

CONTENTS

ACKNOWLEDGMENTS

I feel blessed and give thanks to divine source and my spirit team for the guidance they give and that they use me as an instrument for healing. This has made it possible to bring this information through, allowing this book's publication. I feel deep gratitude and appreciation for my spirit team for their undying love, constant support, and inspiration to keep going.

This book is dedicated to the memory of Richard Comeau, my father, who crossed over in 2016 and taught me to stand on my own two feet, my mother, Rose, and brother, David. At times I'm sure they thought this was a little out there. My mom would courageously allow me the opportunity to work with her, whether using tuning forks, the Melchizedek method, or emotion code and listened.

To my wonderful colleague and friend, Dr. Tony Lebro, who offered me the opportunity to work with him out of his wellness center, A Lebro Center for Well Being, in the Kittery, Maine, and Plaistow, New Hampshire, offices.

And to you, the reader. It was my intention when I started this book to help educate and bring understanding to those who are willing enough to be open and look at the world with new perception.

INTRODUCTION

In the Beginning: Movies and Reading

As a child, I remember movies being a very big part of my life. At the time, computers were nonexistent. I remember how happy I felt watching something imaginative, outside the box. I recall going to the theater and the anticipation of waiting to get a ticket, ordering popcorn, and then sitting through the advertisements before the upcoming movie. It was exciting, knowing as we waited with great expectation that the movie was about to finally begin. There was music in the background, and then at last the lights would start to slowly dim. It all felt like something larger than myself. I could relax and be myself. My imagination could soar. Reading books, including novels, love stories, dramas, murder mysteries, and horror, didn't move me. They actually felt boring and stale. Then, at the age of twenty, I was given a book by Carlos Castaneda. It was very different from anything I had read. And I must say, it shifted me when I read it. It opened me up to researching similar books about dreams, numerology, tarot, psychic phenomena, and UFOs. I read authors such as Ruth Montgomery, Shirley McClain, Delores Cannon, and too many others to mention. That was just the beginning. It opened up a whole new world for me. The list was an endless array of imagination. For a time I studied numerology and took a tarot class as I followed this path into the paranormal and metaphysical.

As I continued on my adventure and new path of learning many new and exciting things, I read everything I could get my hands on in these fields. I would get caught up in what felt like a new, magical world, no longer with just sight but thoughts that would stream through while I was reading. My brain felt like it was always engaged in a happy place. I continued on this new quest as I went through a few loving relationships, or I thought they were, but they never really felt complete, like there was something missing. I remember thinking, *Is this all there is?* The few relationships I had, even the two marriages (one annulled), just dissolved. I learned much about myself from these relationships and their families. I kept searching, but for what? That was the underlying question. "What next?" Alone, I kept moving forward on this new journey I found myself in. And then there was Reiki. It wasn't until one night while meditating that I realized I could "hear" my spirit team speaking to me. My first experience with this sensation was shortly after reading and meeting two sisters and authors of *Angelspeake*, Barbara Marks and Trudy Griswold, in 1998.

Soon after my spirit team came through during one meditation and dropped a seed by saying, "Watch for the lights."

I had no idea what the heck they were referring to, so I prodded them for a little more information. "What lights? Stoplights?"

They simply replied, "Not stoplights. Just pay attention to lights."

I found early on that they don't give a lot of information, just enough to help us pay attention and move us along. After that, I was always on alert. Once I was at a small restaurant while out with friends. We were all sitting at the bar in a restaurant in Andover, Massachusetts, eating, when suddenly the hanging can lights over us started to blink on and off. I politely excused myself and headed to the restroom for a moment of quiet contemplation. Some of my friends noticed but paid little attention and went about their business of having fun.

After becoming centered, I asked spirit, "Is that you flipping the lights at the bar?"

Their reply was, "Yes, indeed. That is us using the lights to get your attention."

From there on, I made it a point to stay connected as much as possible. This was in 1997. And so it continued. This went on pretty regularly for some years, until I got used to them contacting me. I recall another night (when I was only working part time in the holistic field) when I was working at a hotel. It took place while I was taking a break with a guest. This woman and I were having a cup of tea together, and during the break, all the lights in the breakfast room started blinking on and off as they had so many times before. The guest commented on how odd it was that the lights were only flickering in that room. I told her it must be a power surge and politely excused myself. One guess what direction I went? Yes, of course, another trip to the restroom!

I meditated briefly and asked the spirit team, "Is this you again flickering the lights on and off?"

They clearly came through acknowledging that indeed it was to get my attention. As my journey continued, it was now time to move on with me.

Time to Be Me

By this time I was in my early forties and tired of the rat race with relationships. I was ready to sink my teeth into the metaphysical work I so loved. It just felt right! So again I read everything I could on the subject, taught classes, offered clinics, etc. During this time, I was learning to be more myself and less of what society thought I should be. I was starting to care less and less about other people's perceptions of me, my thinking, and my teachings, and just started to be. It became seriously apparent to me I was onto something—something I didn't want to let go of. For a time I continued offering help and knowledge in the ancient healing art of Reiki. I traveled around New England offering my services to anyone in need, from private homes for both people and animals, to volunteering at Elliot Hospital in Manchester, New Hampshire (the drive one way was forty-five minutes), and wellness centers for little to no pay, just to get knowledge of what this was all about and get more experience. The people I met and the experiences were extraordinary. I met so many who had real issues with health and emotional unrest, but they all received genuine relief through this ancient healing. While I was continuously being guided to stay open, tuned in, and connected, meditation helped me progress and stay grounded. I found myself wanting to do more service work, but what I didn't realize was that I was slowly integrating higher frequencies of energy into my work, attracting more, but not consciously aware.

I will jump back in time here for a moment to when I first started meditating in the late '90s. As I mentioned earlier, one night while I was meditating, I realized I could hear my spirit team speak to me. In my first experience and contact with an angel, she called herself Angelica. The second was with an angel who called himself Dennis. The *Angelspeake* books were instrumental in the beginning, helping develop abilities I didn't know I could tap. I learned to be still and quiet and listen, but in the beginning, I had no idea what I was listening to. Here are some tips I learned.

I learned the seven steps to talk with your angels, how to receive messages, how you know it's an angel message, automatic dictation, coping with misses, doubt, anger, and still more. At this time I slowly continued moving along, with my last relationship behind me, and concentrated on me for a change and what I really wanted for myself. It was at that moment that I decided the service of energy balancing was what I was always attracted to and loved. It was now time to pursue it. So I took the inspiration I received and forged forward. With each baby step forward, I felt increasingly different while working with Reiki. Although I enjoyed the work and the results, I had been feeling for some time a sense or urging not to follow such staunch, rigid participation when administering it to the field and maintain a flow. I kept up with it for a few more years and suddenly found myself drawn to sound, including crystal singing bowls and tuning forks! I found myself once again forging down another new path, the mechanics of sound energy. In 2007 I was introduced to tuning forks. I took a class with a gentleman out of California but felt less than inspired after his class. He continuously spoke over our heads about his knowledge and teachings. Shortly after this class, I decided the search was to be continued. There were many in the sound industry I had observed and learned from. I knew what I wanted and didn't want. I just hadn't found the right fit. My experiences taught me well. I wanted someone mindful of science and spirituality, but also presentation! I wanted someone who had a style similar to my own: simplistic, inspiring, educating. That happy medium was key for me. I found what I was looking for. Sometime in 2008, after being introduced to crystal singing bowls, I found a woman out of Vermont who was teaching biofield tuning with tuning forks named Eileen McKusick. As I continued attending sound bath gatherings with the singing bowls, I again studied everything I could on this work in sound. I followed a woman for a time who had been offering sound baths for a number of years and supported her endeavors, learning more all the while. I slowly started to integrate a few bowls into my practice until I could afford all seven bowls needed to offer my own gatherings. I practiced for a year before I felt proficient enough to offer a gathering publicly at my studio in 2009. As I continued down this path of sound, oftentimes feeling like I was on a roller coaster, I would play one or two of the crystal bowls or the tuning forks in my home to meditate.

Hearing Them

One day when I was eighteen years old while driving my little yellow Subaru, it started overheating. I was just leaving an offramp and needed to pull over where it was safe and out of the way. Since I was a bit of a tomboy growing up, I was often around my brother, cousin, and uncles. They were always tinkering with car motors, snowmobiles, and motorcycles. I knew enough of what to do, or so I thought at eighteen! I was in a safe place and hopped out of the vehicle, lifted the hood, and pressed the vacuum cap button on the radiator again and again repeatedly, hearing the steam escape. Now since I was eighteen and wasn't really willing to wait it out, I thought this must be enough time to let most of the steam out and opened the cap. To my surprise, it exploded with a gush of steam all over me! It did spray my face slightly. I was uninjured, but at that moment, I heard a loud gasp of what sounded like a crowd of people around me! I looked around, but there was no one on the street but me.

I thought at that moment, *How strange. What the heck was that? Did I imagine it?* It was my spirit team. Even in those early days, spirit was around and I could hear them. I just didn't know it yet. Now, years later, as I began finding myself offering more and more sound bath gatherings and using the tuning forks, one night at a gathering of singing bowls, an odd occurrence took place. I was well on my way into the evening's event playing seven singing bowls. All was quiet. Everyone was in a meditative state or sleeping. Now I must tell you, I have a keen sense of hearing. I hear things that most do not in a room. This night was different. The spirit team was not going to be using the lights. Something very specific was about to take place.

Before I go any further, let me shed some light on the different states of being. Most importantly, the alpha state is the state one is in during a sound bath or a tuning fork session. These are the five states of being:

- **Gamma**: Being in very high alert, like truck drivers or taking a test
- **Beta**: Being wide awake, daytime
- **Alpha**: In between states, still cognizant of one's surroundings but light
- **Theta**: Being the dream state, not cognizant of one's surroundings
- **Delta**: Very deep, not consciously aware; coma patients are said to resonate at this level

Okay, let's continue. It was in that moment of peaceful bliss I heard a very distinct voice come through saying, "I am Metatron. I am here to work with you."

It was as clear as a conversation I have with anyone standing next to me. So working to compose myself, and pretending like a five-year-old that I didn't hear that voice, I kept playing. Several minutes passed, which seemed like an eternity and moving in slow motion.

I once again heard another voice come through with a bit different tone stating, "I am Melchizedek. I am here to work with you."

Now by this time I was a little freaked out, thinking I must have conjured up an alien or something! I had never heard of these names before. I hadn't fully composed myself from the first voice I heard and still wasn't sure what to make of all this. I'd never asked for names before during any meditations. I didn't really have a desire to know that.

Divine source would always come through saying, "You have a spiritual council, a team that works with you every day, and their guidance to you comes from divine source."

This night was different. Divine source was still guiding my spirit team to work with me, but they came through, giving names this time. Now as time passed, my mind was racing, thinking there was an alien trying to communicate with me. I thought to myself, Oh crap, now what do I do!

It was in that moment that I heard a third voice come through saying, "I am that I am. I am here to work with you, as are they."

Now I'm not a staunchly religious person, but I knew this phrase was Jesus Christ coming through to speak with me. He always said, "I am that I am" with me. I knew in that moment I had not conjured up an alien and was in good hands with whomever Jesus Christ had brought through with him. At the conclusion of the gathering that evening, I asked one of the women there (she was a psychic) if she knew these names.

She replied with wide eyes and surprise and asked, "Yeah, why are you asking that?"

I told her reluctantly what had just happened, and since I didn't know these names, I wondered if she did.

She replied, "Not aliens—far from it. They are archangels and ascended masters."

I thanked her for giving me that information. I had never heard of them or what their rank might be. Metatron[1] and Melchizedek[2] are in the Bible.

This was another beginning on my journey. The Melchizedek method of energy work was about to make its entrance.

---

[1] Metatron is an archangel in Judaism, known as the recording angel or the chancellor of heaven. The name *Metatron* is not mentioned in the Hebrew Bible, nor is it mentioned in the early Enoch literature. He was an angel and the scribe of God who recorded the word of God in heaven. Metatron was personally selected by God to write down his word. He is the third Enoch son of Jared, of the line of Seth, third son of Adam and Eve (Genesis 5:19). This Enoch, who famously "walked with God," is the seventh generation.

[2] Melchizedek in the Old Testament is the king of Salem and a high priest who blessed Abraham after he rescued his nephew Lot from the destruction of Sodom and Gomorrah. Abraham gave him one tenth of his wealth, which is today known as tithing. Genesis is filled with genealogies, but for Melchizedek, there is no record of his lineage, before or after. Melchizedek was a priest in an order that had no beginning. Because Jesus is the order's greatest priest, it will also never end. Jesus is not a Levitical priest for the Israelites but a priest of the order of Melchizedek, meaning he is a priest for all.

PROLOGUE

This book has been in the making for the last three years. As we begin this book, the last years since my father crossed over have been filled with much learning concerning the purpose and direction of my work over the last twenty-one years. There have also been responsibilities I could not have prepared for, including learning to not only hear my spirit team but also to trust and have faith I'm on the correct path for me. I've lived by metaphysical principles, but more than that, I'm sharing what I've learned to help empower and open your mind and to think outside the box, always forging forward, no matter how dark some points in my life felt. This is a journey about evolving and sharing with you how the last twenty-one years in the metaphysical field have helped shape and create positive changes in my life, whether it was things I learned about myself through personal relationships, work associates, and colleagues or being a strong advocate of vegetarian eating with proper foods and nutrition. Since I am an energy practitioner, many of the chapters in this book are about the different modalities I use (which will be explained further into the book) and meditations I've been involved with these last twenty-one years. Some of the information contained in this book is written in a format of questions and answers during those meditations with my spirit team. Now fasten your seat belts as we begin this journey. Stay with me.

Meditation with Elohim
January 29, 2015

We are here with you if you wish to speak with us. We are all here. We are here to tell you that from this point forward, you will now be speaking directly with the Elohim. We will still be here with you, but your conversations will be directly with them, unless they feel there is a message you need to hear from us. Now with all that said, that is why we told you there were many things taking place behind the scenes. We will now have you in direct dialogue from here with the Elohim. We are still here watching, helping.

Meditation with Elohim
March 9, 2015

Comment: Please explain to me again the Elohim and universal divine source.

Elohim: The divine supreme source is made up of the Elohim Council. It is not two separate beings. Let us continue. The Elohim Council is made up of an intelligence of light beings that make up the divine supreme being. We are not separate; we unite together as the one. We make up the Godhead collectively. The divine supreme source and Elohim Council is not the hundred and forty-four thousand. That is a group of light beings but not the Elohim.

Comment: So you, the Elohim Council, make up the divine source. Is that correct? You are not a separate council from the divine source. Is that correct?

Elohim: That is precisely correct.

It has come to our attention that your energies are a little low from all the clearing you did this weekend. Take it easy today. Do something for you today. You will be hearing from the people in your meditation healing last evening. You sent out a lot of energy during that session. We are here to work with you. You will start to see more attention coming to you for your work. No one knew what you were about until now. It is good. You have exceeded your expectation. You are moving forward into new territory.

CHAPTER 1

Melchizedek and Spirit Team Coming Through

Spirit Team: *Divine child of God, it is time for you. As we continue this morning, you will notice things about your surroundings. Notice this—they are going to shift. You will see things differently. The things you would normally take for granted, you will notice. As we continue, notice the surroundings shifting you. You're slipping more into the fifth-dimension frequency. You will need the tuning fork work. The Melchizedek work helped a lot this morning. The forks are still needed for much static buildup. As we continue, the book we are helping you put together is needed. As we continue to work together, more information will come through. Love, love, love. Continue to think on these lines. It helps to pull you up. Metatron and Melchizedek are the foundation for the work you are about to bring out. It is important that we talk about the work you are doing presently. Reiki was the foundation to start everything, then sound and Melchizedek. At this juncture we'd like to concentrate on the Melchizedek work for a moment. This work has helped you continue much work. It is time to go over a bit more in that realm. The forms of low vibration and high vibration are converging at this time.*

Q: With free will divine source, why can't you take all as they are and simply remove what's not needed and converge?

1

A: Once you have more understanding of these realms, you'll understand. So let's continue. In the book there are things we need to go over with you. This book will help many. The star seeds are here to help. Love is all around you. Stay with it.

Q: In Ruth Montgomery's books, her team came through each morning starting right away and had names. How do I refer to you, as the spiritual team or something else?

A: You will refer to us in the book as the spiritual team, and there are many of us.

Q: Where are you all from—the same dimension, etc.?

A: We are all from the eighth dimension. We know that more understanding will come to you.

Q: So where do the Pleiadeans come from? Is it the same dimension?

A: The Pleiadeans are a life form. We are not. We are energy, with no form.

Q: Okay, understood. So where specifically do they reside? A planet, a dimension, etc.?

A: They reside in a completely different galaxy than your own.

Q: Do we know this galaxy?

A: No, this is uncharted as yet.

Q: Okay is there a way to measure distance from us, longitude, latitude, light years, etc.?

A: It is light years upon light years away.

Q: You once told me about zoning out and that we are slipping in and out of the fifth-dimension frequency. Are you talking about all humans who have a high frequency doing this or just talking about myself at the moment?

A: All. There were many asteroids that destroyed much of the planet they lived on. They were able to migrate to another. They have watched the human race for centuries. They have grown as a race and desired to help. They have worked with many humans. They wish to continue conversing with you.

Q: What is the difference between Hathors and Pleiadeans?

A: Pleiadeans are more advanced technologically. Hathors work in the eighth-dimension frequency and are free of form.

Q: Have the Hathors come to speak with me in this lifetime?

A: Yes, many times. They frightened you. You were not ready

Q: I remember meditating one night many years ago when a group wanted to speak with me, but they would not give their group name or anything about themselves. Was that the Hathors?

A: No, it was not. There are many such life forms that wish to speak with humans.

Q: So why did they not wish to speak of who they were?

A: They were highly evolved beings. They simply wanted to make contact with you.

Q: So let me get this straight in my mind. It's okay for these life forms to come through and not give us info about themselves and possibly frighten us. My question is, why come? Why bother?

A: They do not wish to frighten, only to open your awareness.

Q: There's been so much talk through the years here about negative energy, dark forces, low-vibration frequencies, etc. There have been horror movies, books, and much more. We live in a duality of positive and negative. Are there low vibrations in other dimensions, galaxies, etc., that can and do try to connect with us?

A: *My dear child of God, these are very good questions. It is for this reason that this book needs to come out. In answer to your question, yes and no. There are low vibration, as you put it, that have evolved as the human race has but that are still learning also. So to help with the understanding of this, for instance, some with low vibration from outside your galaxy reside with no form and still others have form.*

Q: *What distinguishes the difference?*

A: *Evolution. Everything grows at its own pace.*

Q: *So the low-vibration beings from outside our galaxy and dimension, are they lower than our own frequency?*

A: *Very good question. They are not, but there must always be a balance in the universe. There are progression levels. Do you understand?*

Q: *I do. So at this moment in time, am I speaking with my spirit team, Pleiadeans, or another?*

A: *You are with your spirit council, your team. They consist of humans who have crossed over throughout time, not just this lifetime, but also angels, archangels, and ascended beings.*

Q: *What is the difference between ascended beings and ascended masters as we term them here? Are they one and the same?*

A: *Yes, correct.*

Q: *Okay, what group does HEB (Highly Evolved Beings) fall into?*

A: *The HEB fall into the category of eighth dimension and above.*

Q: *So the Pleiadeans fall into this council?*

A: *Pleiadeans do not. They are still of form. As we continue, there is much to discuss.*

Q: *A thought comes to me to ask about the so-called Bigfoot being that many say they have had a glimpse of. My information on this* came through some years ago. It is highly evolved and is here to witness and observe and can travel between realms at a moment's notice. Is this the case?

A: It is. They have been here for a very long time. And as you were told, that is the reason they have not been captured by humans.

Q: Can they cloak themselves so as not to be seen, but are still in the third dimension?

A: Cloaking they cannot do. They slip in and out of dimensions. They do not wish to harm, only observe.

Q: Why have they taken on such a primitive appearance?

A: They wish to remain neutral, invisible while here.

Q: Are they taking notes? Do they reference our behavior on some platform for learning or educating?

A: They observe to research. They are a particular race from outside this dimension of 3D.

Q: Is this what they look like where they reside?

A: It is not.

Q: Okay, so this now gets into dimensions as well as galaxies. What is the difference?

A: Dimensions are in all galaxies, all universes.

Q: I don't even know where to begin. Is there a particular number of dimensions per galaxy, per universe?

A: Good question. There are an infinite number of dimensions throughout. As we continue, there is one last thing we'd like to discuss with you. Take time for you.

Q: Show me the way to stay in the flow and manifest better.

A: You have the ability to. We will help. It's positive intention that comes through the good for all humanity. You are on the right path.

Once the book comes out, people will look upon you differently. They will tell you it helped explain things to them easily, helped them move along with difficulties they were having, and helped them understand energy work. We are here to work with you. We will continue. Until next time. Love to you, divine child of God.

CHAPTER 2

Symptoms and Food

Spirit Team: *Some symptoms will be regulated by food. As we begin this morning's session, we would like to start with your book. It will have several chapters. As we begin, you will start to see sequences take shape. What we want to work on this morning are attributes or abilities. These are abilities individuals will start to see in themselves but are unsure of where to research or look into. As we continue, each person's ability will be unique unto him or herself. Some may find they have a knack for writing but were afraid to start. It could be something as simple as poetry. As we continue, there will be many who feel shiftings in their systems that they do not understand. These symptoms could be headaches, aches and pains for no apparent reason, nausea, dizziness, lightheadedness, tingling sensations, and ringing in the ears. These are just symptoms of the energy shifting throughout the system. As we continue, those are just a few. The important thing to keep in mind is to be sure to get sleep, rest, stay hydrated, and eat lighter. It is important to stay with vegetables and fruits and consume as little sugar as possible. The calories we're not as concerned with as much as carbohydrates and sugar. Organic food and non-GMO foods are most important. Do the best you can to switch up to these. Go slow, but work to make the effort. It will help bring the system on board easier. As we continue, this chapter will be dedicated to symptoms. The* food intake will be closely associated with the blood and its ability to fuel the system.

Q: What is the difference between eating mammals and fish. I know it has to do with DNA.

A: The DNA strands of fish are similar to that of humans. The DNA potentiality is higher. If one is a vegetarian and consumes meat from mammals, it lowers one's frequency, but more, it shifts the potentiality. It reverts to primal man. When one doesn't eat meat, the potential is greater to move forward. The fuel one puts into the system will decide how the body will regulate itself. Love, love, love is all around you. You are becoming more involved, more in sync with your destiny. As we continue the food source, what they can grow their own is key. There are a few ways to grow foods simply. A small plot in one's yard, on a deck, and the hydroponics that are now available are very effective. There are many ways to grow one's own food at a fraction of the cost of buying it once one is in a rhythm. As we continue, greens are most important, but mix them with others. The nutrients are important to the body.

Q: A friend and colleague once mentioned to me that her doctor suggested not to eat greens while she was on certain medications. This will be something to consider, as people listen to their doctors like God.

A: There are still going to be fruits and vegetables one can eat while on medication. Just because one cannot eat certain greens does not mean to eliminate them all. Good question.

Sugar is the number-one insult to the physical body with regard to food. It is important to curb it as much as possible. Consider cutting down or stopping altogether. This will be challenging but not impossible. With anything the body is addicted to, there is a challenge to release from it, for example, nicotine in cigarettes, caffeine in coffee, cocaine and other recreational drugs, prescription drugs, etc.

CHAPTER 3

Moving Forward

Spirit Team: *We are here with you, divine child of God. It gives us great pleasure to be with you. As we continue at this juncture, we will talk briefly about how to move forward. The title for this Chapter will be "Moving Forward." As we proceed, briefly we'd like to speak about the challenges one faces in staying with it and meditating daily when possible. Remain vigilant with food intake and exercise the body—move it. Be outside as much as possible. This chapter will help people let go of old patterns, old perceptions. As we begin to explore new territory, you will experience waves of energy moving through you. As you start to explore new reaches in your work. You will see new freedom come from this. The love you feel for your peers is extraordinary. Stay in tune with that. As we continue, we want you to start to recognize your abilities. Your abilities are starting to reveal themselves to you. Stay in touch with them. Do not boohoo this. It is happening. Much is taking place planet-wide now and not all negative. There is much taking place that is positive. Stay tuned in to these. You do well to maintain this. Stay with it. Lower-vibration individuals who have not learned or awakened yet to the high consciousness still feel the need to control and manipulate others with their own perceptions. One will need to listen very closely to the gentle stirrings within. As each individual starts to shift, he or she will be better able to hear and receive direction on* *his or her path. As we continue, meditating of a simple nature will help. Sit still in quiet contemplation or silently listen to soft, gentle melodies. As you have already suggested to many, ten minutes a day is a good place to begin. Do it more as time allows. It's important to allow this time in one's day. This will help guide one on one's journey. It's through meditation or quiet contemplation the direction comes. So for starters, if one were to take a walk, that is quiet contemplation. Sitting in a vehicle silently or with calming music during the day at one's workplace is also helpful. These are starting points to bring one to the application of quiet stillness. As we continue, there will come a time when one will know one is ready and can handle the stillness of meditation with no music, just quiet listening. Listening—we use this word loosely. One will have messages coming through one energetically, one's vibration. One may feel this as a surge of energy or have sense of wellbeing, lightness. As you continue now, think of a time when you knew something but didn't know why. That's the vibrations coming through the system, activating the senses of intuition, your all-knowing and understanding.*

As we continue, we would like to close this chapter by suggesting a practice. If one is ready to move forward on the journey of learning, this will help. Take time to breathe, but not like at a gym while working out. Be consciously aware of your breath, using slow, full breathing. This can be done with great effectiveness in the car, at the work place, in a restroom, or at home when situations become heated. Breathe. Take a break from any situation for a few moments. Take deep, slow breaths and repeat: "I am okay. I am all right. This will pass."

CHAPTER 4

Surroundings and Inspiration

Spirit Team: It is good that you did a tuning fork session on yourself; it was needed. As you move forward, we would like to talk to you about the book. This is something you need to stay with now. It's always a pleasure to work with your energies. You are eager and help yourself, making it easier for us to help. As we continue now, the book is going to be very important. There will be a few chapters we will discuss at length the subject matter therein. The book will help many people who are struggling to move forward. It is at this time we say to you, "It is time." We'd like to continue now with surroundings and watchful things around you that can be of inspiration. As we continue, one receives inspiration from nature or surroundings that moves one forward. We'd also like to go over grounding. It is important for one to wear proper attire. Grounding shoes or being barefoot when possible is key, along with meditation. Keep in mind the love of nature, being outside, and in particular being around trees. We'd like to discuss time spent in nature. This chapter will be helpful in people's ability to understand. At this time, consider taking a walk on the beach, reading a book outdoors, taking a pet out for a walk, or bike riding. Whatever one can do to be outdoors will help with intuition. It will help open one's consciousness. It's a slow progression, a starting point, but be ever mindful of consistency. Another aspect we'd like to discuss is swimming and being in water or near it. Water is an important factor we do not wish to omit. Stay in touch with water, whether on a boat, on a dock, or by the waters' edge. Dangle your feet in the water and make contact. There are many benefits of sitting peacefully in or around water. Swimming fully immersed, of course, is most beneficial. So in moving forward, there are things that can be done that help the process. All work in conjunction with each other, but it's never limited to one aspect. Find the one that works best, but also break it up. Don't use the same procedure over and over. Diversify, stretch the self, and always try something new. Even if it doesn't work out, it's in the journey that we continue to learn. One may learn some aspect of the self one was not aware of simply by trying something new. Perspective is how we view things. The more open we are to learning, the more progress we make in moving forward.

CHAPTER 5

What's Next

Spirit Team: We know we discussed diversity and grounding, but let's start by how you'll put your work together. As you begin a new chapter in your life, it's time to move along a more defined playing field. Let's begin with the next chapter of your life. As you move forward, there will be changes in how people observe you. Once the book is published, it will change people's perception of you. They will look at you with different eyes. And for us, we say it's about time. This is the beginning of something much larger than you are able to imagine. So as we continue, let's focus on what's next. In this book, you have covered a lot of territory. Let's continue now with you and how the story unravels. You have stepped away from conventional living. It began with your imagination opening as a young girl, your experiences, and now it continues with educating the public and how they can better move along their journey. This will be an extension of you. How do we better help people educate themselves to move forward, to become unstuck? We have talked about a good many things—galaxies, dimensions, Pleiadeans, Hathors, eighth-dimension light beings and still more. Where do we go from here? We would like to speak to you about the emotion code work and the Melchizedek work. When we began putting this book together with you, you had experiences with some of these, so let's start to integrate more. We will give a breakdown of some of these works so people have a better understanding of them. Let's start with Reiki. This modality helped many people open up to the idea that there is something much larger than themselves to tap into and that they can work with. Energy has many forms: trees, rocks, grass, animals, people, planets, etc. Reiki was just the start. As we will explain, Reiki is a fourth-dimension frequency that helps open the conscious mind, a doorway so to speak. This doorway has led many people down a path of enlightenment. The Melchizedek method is fifth-dimension frequency. It is like no other healing modality. It works through the body to the DNA layer. It encompasses many layers. As we bring that frequency through, it not only releases what doesn't serve the individual but also heightens his or her vibration. It works with the DNA strands on an individual level. There are many facets to the Melchizedek frequency. You are just becoming involved in the emotion code, which uses magnets. It's much like the tuning fork work you're involved in. It will be of interest. It is very powerful and effective. People who come to you for energy balancing will be from all walks of life with a host of different ailments, from physical to emotional. Like the tuning forks, it is a release of stuck energy but of deep-seated, trapped emotions. Also, the magnets will release from the individual's inherited stuck energy that is not his or her own but is inherited from a parent, grandparent, great-grandparent, and much beyond that into ancestral genealogy. It releases from the individual and the ancestor it originated from, no matter how far back it goes. But it also releases the trapped emotion from all ancestors who brought it through generations! Each modality will help the many, as no two people are the same. What you express to the individual about trying to find the right modality is key. Encourage others not to become disheartened after starting their journey. It is about finding the right connection for each individual. As you have pointed out on many occasions, what works for one may not work for another.

CHAPTER 6

Meditation

Spirit Team: Meditation is the awakening of the conscious and subconscious mind and no longer being separate. The subconscious mind and the conscious mind are ready to forge forward, to blend, so to speak. That takes time and practice. There are many who are ready to do just that. It's through meditation and energy balancing that one's vibration can shift. It's in the silence of meditation that we *hear* through the cells. It has been challenging for the human to sit and be still in the silence, until now. Many are ready, and more will follow. Let's talk a little about meditation. There are many forms of meditation. Many religions offer forms of meditation. We want to be clear—it is in the silence and breath, to be still and listen and not just with the 3D hearing but by tuning in. It's like being a radio receiver. Once you've connected with the frequency that matches your own, you are tuned in. It is in this silence that we move forward. There is much taking place in those moments. Cells are being nourished, including tissues and bones. All are in tune with something larger than themselves. As we wake from our slumber, we actually change the frequency of the human being. One hears much more than with the human ear. The entire body is focused on something larger than itself. It is in those moments that we learn, in the silence. As we continue, we would like to bring you to a place of knowing. In the beginning when starting meditation, one may

16

be restless, antsy, fidgety, almost uncomfortable. It takes practice, and one must limit oneself to short periods daily. We suggest ten minutes a day to start, as you have suggested, but at the same time each day. As you are aware, during meditation, the body slows down. The mind, the cells, and blood pressure level. The body becomes more balanced and comfortable in time. Let's talk briefly about the in-between phase of meditations. The in-between is where a person feels like he or she is not here in the now—like he or she is floating and is much lighter, not heavy. This is when people start to really connect to universal source, divine source, divine source council, God, whatever one's term is. It's in these moments that they feel very connected and comfortable. When the time is right, one will connect with one's own team or council. It's in those moments that they will have an epiphany. The connection can be made, and one will hear with different ears. As we continue, we would like to start another chapter. We will call it, "Pleiadeans and Astral Travel."

CHAPTER 7

Pleiadeans and Astral Travel

Spirit Team: As you continue with the book, it gives us great pleasure to speak with you. You have learned much in the last year. We would like to speak about the Pleiadeans. They have been around you for some time. As we continue, the Pleiadeans would like to start communicating with you. They have asked us to help initiate conversation with you. We believe you are ready to connect. They have much to teach you, and there is much you can share at this time.

Q: Is this communication going to be much like what we do together?

A: They are physical form like yourself and can appear.

Q: What is it exactly they would like to discuss?

A: It's about time travel or astral travel.

Q: What? Did I hear you correctly—time travel?

A: Yes indeed you have.

Q: Time travel—what does that mean exactly?

A: Just as it says. They would like to show you it can be achieved, much like the conversation we had some time ago about Bigfoot and how they do this.

Okay, so as we pick this up where we left off, it is in your highest good to pay close attention. The words are important. We were speaking to you about astral travel or time travel, which is the next subject. It is thought-provoking and possible. As we move forward, these are things people will find interesting. As we begin, astral travel is not new. It is just a matter of moving energy from one place to another.

Q: You mentioned that Bigfoot travels between dimensions. Is that the same that you are referring to here?

A: Yes. Moving energy is simply unwinding the mind. When one is meditating, the energy takes one to another space, another frequency.

It is there that we begin to let go of the conscious mind and simply be. You've heard of astral projection. This is what time travel or astral travel is about—moving energy from one place to another. It is entirely possible as many have done this on a regular basis. There is also something called remote viewing that you are familiar with. That too is moving energy to see something in another location. Again, it's simply energy. Now let us explain. As one begins one's journey into the metaphysical, it starts with simple things—for example, yoga, tai chi, meditation, Reiki etc. As one progresses and begins to have energy adjustments to one's field of energy, one shifts. One becomes comfortable with the notion of trying more. In that moment, one steps over the threshold of the linear timeline to time travel. Linear time is the conscious mind living day to day. Stepping outside that realm speeds up the mind to something much larger than linear time. You have a question.

Q: I thought the book was to help educate people about things they could put to use on a daily basis

A: This information is to help open people's conscious awareness—to think outside the box, so to speak.

Q: And you think astral travel (time travel) is something to help people on a daily basis?

A: It is to help people open up to more than what's directly in front of them. This is not something all will be using or will want to. Again, it's only to help open the conscious mind to accept more.

Okay, as we continue, they would like to discuss this with you to add to your book. It's about raising one's vibration to such a level that the physical body is not needed, temporarily

Q: Okay, I'm listening.

A: It is entirely possible if a person's body amperage is fast enough.

Q: Fast enough? What exactly does that mean?

A: If a human body's vibration rate moves fast enough, the light body within takes over. It's like the example you use in demonstrating the wings of a hummingbird. That's a great analogy. The faster they move, the less you see them. It is for that reason some can see and some cannot. As you continue to interact with the Pleiadeans, they will teach you much. It is for this reason that we wish to speak to you at this time. Shall we continue?

Q: Yes.

A: As we move on, there is much we will cover at this time. For starters, it is in your highest good to stop with any heavy foods. They slow you down.

Q: You mentioned a person would need to raise their vibration enough so the inner light body could transition out. How does one accomplish this?

A: Very good question. Certain foods have more nutrients than others. Some have higher vibrations than others. Meditation also elevates one's vibration.

Q: I understand, but one would need to be doing a lot more than meditation and eating certain foods for that to take place. What else aren't you mentioning?

A: Very good question. Other methods are exercise and being outdoors, and when we say outdoors, we mean near natural vegetation and water.

Q: And still I get all that, but there's still more you're not mentioning. The reason I ask is because if every person who meditated and all vegetarians of the world and nature lovers were doing this, there would be many already doing this. So there must be more.

A: We can tell you it takes great dedication and practice. This can be done. One needs to be ready. As you continue to move forward now on your journey, there is only one subject the Pleiadeans would like to discuss with you.

Q: What else are they interested in discussing?

A: We'll have them come through to speak with you soon. There will be a meeting of the minds. The information they give and teach you will help many. This is all for now. We will speak with you soon. Divine child of God, we love you. It gives us great pleasure to speak with you. Love to you, child.

Next Day

Q: Okay, is there more you'd like to bring to light on this subject for people to understand?

A: Yes, very good question. It has been brought to our attention that there will be an opportunity for you to witness this firsthand. The

Pleiadeans would like the opportunity to meet and discuss more things on this subject.

Q: They have a form of their own. Is it much like human form?

A: It is entirely similar to your own. They have a slim body structure. They are taller, and their eyes a bit larger than your own.

They are a very kind and gentle life form. They have been to your planet many times to help. They have been where your species is and wish to offer help and nothing more. They observe and offer help where needed, but not to expose who they are or why they are here to everyone. It would frighten those who are not ready.

Q: What have they learned from observing us?

A: That you are a kind species but still limited. That you long for more but do not know how to reach it. That your species will go to great lengths to help others, but on a singular level, you are afraid to help the self.

Q: Do they have abilities beyond our own?

A: Yes, they have learned much and are willing to share.

Q: Are you at liberty to name a few?

A: They can move between dimensions, like Bigfoot. They can move objects with thought very easily using telekinesis.

As we continue with this conversation, you are learning as we speak. It is important for you to continue with your meditations. You have done well. Let's continue. As you wake each morning, that is the best time for you to interact. Your energies are higher. You are more receptive. As we continue, we would like to discuss more. It has come to our attention that it is time for you meet the Pleiadeans.

Q: Are they male and female genders like ourselves?

A: They have gender.

Q: *Do they procreate as humans do?*

A: *They do, but not in the same manner. That is another subject that we will cover at a later time.*

Q: *Do they look like humans?*

A: *Yes, they do.*

Q: *Do they have hands, feet, fingers, toes, etc.?*

A: *Yes.*

Q: *Okay, so why do they want a meeting at this time?*

A: *They are here to help. They wish to give you information for your book to help your civilization.*

Q: *I'm not at liberty with free time at the moment, as I'm the caretaker of my mother, who has dementia and cannot be left unattended. I do some work outside the home in an office.*

A: *It is our pleasure to work at your convenience.*

Q: *Okay, so with whom am I speaking at the moment?*

A: *You are still with your divine spirit team. We are here with the Pleiadeans. We have spoken, and they are ready to speak with you.*

Q: *Do they have hair on their heads?*

A: *Not as a rule, but if it makes you feel more comfortable, then they can.*

Q: *While here with us, do they take on human form or keep their own?*

A: *Very good question. They keep their own form.*

Q: *What color are their eyes?*

A: *They have an indigo shade to them.*

Q: *Do they eat food like us?*

A: *They do, and they expel it in the same manner.*

Q: *So they have kidneys and bladders to expel urine and a colon to expel solid waste from the system.*

A: *They do, but not in the way your human body works.*

CHAPTER 8

Energies

Spirit Team: *As we move on, we would like to discuss another topic: energies. The energies one carries can slow down the progress of moving forward if they become too heavy. The energy stagnates and becomes heavy. That's when the physical body becomes ill. The energy in the body moves slowly, causing the organs' vibration and speed to move more slowly, creating disease in the system and eventual discord or lack of harmony within. The harmonious state of being is crucial for the human being to expand its consciousness. As one becomes interested in taking care of the self, a spark is ignited. It is at that moment that the subconscious mind is activated on a linear timeline. It opens to us. As one meditates and listens, it moves one's frequency in the stillness, the quiet. It's in the silence one hears. It can become deafening at times once we have become better connected.*

Moving forward, we'd like to discuss something else with you. It is inevitable that people will ask how long the human race has been moving forward. How long have they truly been on a path of moving forward since World War I, World War II, the Civil War, Vietnam, etc.? The answer is, "Since the beginning of time." The frequency at this level (3D) is slow and heavy. It takes time for enlightenment. Enlightenment comes to those who persist even in their darkest hour. They hold faith in something larger than themselves. When one holds faith in that thought, one continues to move forward. It's when one stops believing one is better than what's taking place in these dark moments that one stagnates. It's in stagnation and disbelief that one remains in neutral, building heavy vibration frequency in and around themselves. The way to move forward is through love. First and foremost, one must love the self before one can understand and love others. We're certain many have heard the phrase, "Love thyself." As we move on, we would like to discuss another topic: other beings.

CHAPTER 9

Other Beings

Spirit Team: Everything vibrates at a specific frequency, a vibration. This includes absolutely everything—rocks, grass, trees, furnishings in a home, bridges, cars, ships, trains, animals, insects, planets, etc. Well, you get the idea. Everything is connected and has its own unique frequency of knowledge. This brings us to other beings, light beings, and dark beings. The universe is quite expansive and houses many life forms that visit this place of existence. Many beings have visited this planet for thousands of years. Some are here to help and others to observe. As one becomes more acquainted with the self, one becomes lighter, less fearful. In becoming lighter, one moves more fluidly in life. When we become enlightened through work on the self, we are ready to open to the notion of more than just the human race. One begins to change one's perception. One looks at the world with different eyes that are more loving. It is with great understanding that one moves forward at a different pace. As you continue to write, you will see more will come through. It is for your highest good that we break at this moment. Love is always with you. We will continue.

As we move on, we would like to discuss another topic: the new earth.

CHAPTER 10

The New Earth

Spirit Team: The new earth is a fifth-dimension frequency.

Q: The new earth—is it a planet?

A: It is a planet but in another dimension. There will be many who won't be ready and others who won't want to go.

Q: Why would they not want to go?

A: They will still be attached to things here.

Q: Are you referring to people or things?

A: Not just people. In 2003, things started to change more noticeably. There are two earths. The new earth is in a new dimension. The present earth is evolving. With us or without us, it is evolving. It is also a living being and is growing. The symptoms of energy shifts include dizziness, nausea, aches and pains, high blood pressure, heart problems, depression, and joint pain. The body is shifting. Eat live foods, lighter foods, and organic vegetables raw. Stay away from sugar. Drink lots and lots of water. You can't change all at once. It causes too much strain on the system. Drink smoothies. The body does not die to go to the New Earth. You will have the same body with no sickness.

CHAPTER 11

Love and Forgiveness—Very Powerful Frequencies

Spirit Team: We will be giving instructions. These are things needed in the book. There is much coming to you soon, and this will help. Let us start by saying it gives us great pleasure to work with your energies. We are here to work with your energies this morning. Your energies are a little low. We're opening some meridian lines so the chi can flow better. You had a few blocks. As we begin, know your heart is in the right place. This morning we'd like to talk to you about where you are going. Your life up till now has taken you through many twists and turns. That is about to shift up. As we continue, there is a new frequency you are able to attract. It is for this reason things are now changing and shifting for you. You are ready to receive. It has taken time to come to this juncture. There was much you wanted to learn and experience. It's time to move on now from struggle and strife and just be. As we continue, in your book you are to include the topics of love and forgiveness. These are extraordinary frequencies. They are very powerful and fulfilling. Many do not know how to let go of pain and emotional wounds, as it were. You have a knack for helping people come into understanding. We are here to show you the way. In the book you will also need to include words of wisdom of the heart. Key words and phrases people can use on a daily basis are love, forgiveness, help, smile, listen, join, and be happy. As we continue with some phrases, it is in your highest good to jot down as much as you can. Soon you will see a shift of energy to a great degree. Life will change soon. Your life will change. We're not talking about worldly changes at the moment. As we continue now, let it be known that you understand you will be an instrument in bringing information through for this book. Life will shift for you soon.

Q: Are you referring to before the book coming out or after?

A: Your book will change many things for you, but we are talking about changes before the book.

Q: Is there anything in particular you bring through here for information that will be helpful for understanding?

A: It gives us great pleasure to work with your energies. The shift we are referring to is the shift in energies. You will feel the impact when this takes place. You will see a shift of energy in yourself. Your family will shift as well, but differently. They will not understand. We are here to help.

Q: Are they leaving?

A: No, they still have things they wanted to learn.

Q: Are they learning?

A: Yes, but slowly.

You will move forward. This will catapult you in a new direction. They will not understand the changes, but they will see the changes in you. You will be all right. When the shift takes place, you will know. You will know your place. The change is upon you. There have been delays right along, but it is inevitable. It will take place.

It's a shift in the human body. The DNA is shifting. You already have many have more strands. The human race is evolving. As you continue to progress forward and process, you will see things differently. You will have kind eyes that are softer, quieter. As we continue, we have some phrases for you:

- *Love thyself.*
- *Be with the self.*
- *Happiness is yours if you wish for it.*
- *Much success is but only a thought away.*
- *I am all I need to be.*
- *Love is here to stay.*
- *Walk in the light.*
- *Listen and love.*

We will leave you for now. This needs to be continued. Return to it today.

Continued the following day:

Q: Do you wish to continue where we left off? I couldn't get back as I would have liked, sooner than later.

A: Yes, we are very pleased. We would like to pick up where we left off.

As we begin today, we want to say there are very turbulent static frequencies about you. You need tuning forks.

Q: I did use one of the weighted forks this morning and yesterday. That must help some. It was 93.96Hz. Is that correct?

A: That particular fork is for very specific work. It is used for lymphatic fluid.

Q: Anything else it's used for?

A: It's primarily to shift fluids in the body.

Divine child of God, we know you've had much to contend with. We are here to help. As you've seen, this is giving you more inspiration. You have been inspired, moved. There is much coming to you.

CHAPTER 12

Thirty-Six Frequencies

Meditation with Elohim
September 2, 2015
Melchizedek Healing and Resonance Clearing

There are thirty-six frequencies a human being vibrates at, although they don't generally utilize them all. You were looking for the combination for mates. There are three frequencies that need to match.

Diatonic Scale

- *Solar Plexus: E note/528Hz*
- *Heart: F note/341.3Hz*
- *Brain: A note/426.7Hz*
- *Throat: G note/384Hz*

For me, the throat and heart are close. It just depends on instrument I'm playing, crystal bowls or tuning forks. I tend to resonate with the throat more, on many occasions.

Q: How do we know what frequencies these are so we can be sure our mate matches? In other words, how do we figure out what we are vibrating at in these areas?

A: Very good question. The lower earth frequencies are the chakras: C, D, E, F, G, A, and B.

To start with, which of these do you resonate with?

Comment: E, G, and A.

A: Now figure out what those frequencies are in Hz. Those are the three you resonate to. Check your zen tambour notes (similar to a hang drum). Which of these do you resonate with? Then figure out the Hz frequency.

Okay, as we continue, you had many frequencies that didn't resonate any longer, that were old or dense. We removed thirteen of the thirty-six frequencies and replaced them with new frequencies. They are the same frequency, but new.

Q: And how was this accomplished?

A: We simply cut each cord one at a time and replaced them as we worked through you.

Q: Anything further?

A: Just watch the subtle shifting taking place. You will notice changes. Drink lots of water. We will leave you for now.

The next three chapters will be on the mechanics of the modalities I work with.

CHAPTER 13

Biofield Tuning with Tuning Forks

Biofield tuning a sound therapy method using tuning forks that tap into energy patterns and natural rhythms of the body. It's a physics-based approach in assisting the body's ability to heal itself using coherent frequencies. They locate and correct distortions in and around the body's energy field, producing subtle to profound energy shifts and healing effects. Tuning forks use audible acoustic frequencies to balance the body's electrical system but on a much deeper level. They lift one's vibration, clearing away stuck ripples of energy that were created through challenges in one's lifetime, becoming dense and heavy. By lifting the frequency of the distorted vibration, bringing it back to one's own unique frequency, and integrating it through the system, balance and entrainment are restored. Tuning forks were introduced in the 1600s but weren't taken seriously till about the 1700s, when they were used as medicinal healing tools along with magnets.

Some History of Tuning Forks

In 1684, German physician G. C. Schelhammer tried using a common cutlery fork to enhance the experiments that Cardano and

Capivacci were working on. In 1711, twenty-seven years later, in England, royal trumpeter John Shore created the first tuning fork based on Schelhammer's discovery using a common cutlery fork. It was made of steel and had a pitch of A423.5Hz. In 1800, German physicist E.F.F. Chladni, along with others, constructed a complete musical instrument based on sets of tuning forks.

In 1834, J.H. Scheibler presented a set of fifty-four tuning forks ranges from 220Hz to 440Hz. Jammed energy creates pain and swelling. Working with this energy can speed healing and alleviate discomfort. Many people live in a constant state of tension that causes the adrenal glands to become overworked. By releasing unhealthy energetic connections from them and tuning the vibrations, the quality of life and health can be enhanced. Relationships between people and the relationship between people and their animal companions are also energy. Those energy connections can be tuned. This process can assist in the release of fear and anger and create more harmony. We have two bodies: electro-magnetic biofield and physical. A depleted field will slow the body down, although there may not be pathological disease present. The energy field acts like a blueprint of the physical body. Sooner or later a depleted, unbalanced field will create problems in the physical body. It makes sense to correct imbalances before they become a physical condition. With tuning forks, the tones change in pitch when moved they are around the body, in response to information they encounter. These are useful in places that are congested, such as muscle knots, tension in the sciatic nerve, etc. The audible frequencies are beneficial for balancing the nervous system, relaxing muscles and soft tissues. A symptom in the body has a corresponding distortion within the field. When a distortion is located, it can be corrected and brought to an *orderly, balanced frequency pattern. The sound waves penetrate the body and create space between the molecules in a way that's similar to the use of infrasonic frequencies, such as breaking up kidney stones. They intersect with the acoustic vibrations of the body, allowing the forks to find specific static charges, incoherence, and distortion in the field and then balance the body's electrical system. Tuning forks help balance and harmonize distorted frequencies that are found by raising, clearing, and smoothing vibrations! These sessions help reduce inflammation and pain, help people feel more relaxed and rejuvenated, and work the left and right side (yin and yang) and then the ground.*

Tuning Water with Tuning Forks
February 2018

I decided to help Tune Water after a personal tuning fork session on myself. As I tuned-in to a bath of Epsom Salt water, I mentioned I would like to help release rubbish, abuse and trashing it has endured etc... to help release tensions and bring coherence. That I also would like to ease the tensions of all creatures (plant, amphibian, mammal) that lived in that housing.

As I tuned-in to the water, it fully acknowledged it was receptive. (felt like "male" energy) It mentioned it could feel the intensity of my energy through the fork. Saying it felt at times like a tidal wave, then would calm down and feel very gentle like a sublet ripple coming and going. I could actually feel at points, the water swelling like waves in an ocean. Almost like it was breathing...

As we continued, it acknowledged it felt Lighter and was very grateful for the help I had chosen to offer. As we were nearing closure it spoke, saying it remembered me on one of its coastlines. (another occasion, envisioned myself at one of the beaches I would frequent in New Hampshire). I replied I would return to help. Always get goosebumps when I tune-in to things.

We are truly all connected....

Tuning Water with Tuning Forks
April 14 2018

I did a Tuning on water again primarily Ocean, Whales & Dolphins a couple months ago and doing another today. Many that know me, know I'm an advocate for illustrations and demonstrations being very visual in my teachings. I researched a few sites to find an image that was close to what I saw in my mind's eye as I approached. I asked the Whales & Dolphins if I could work with them again as before using the Tuning Forks. Their response was jumping out of the water and standing straight up under the water. I felt them extend great gratitude with my return and their acknowledgment of remembering my vibration. Here is what I saw in my minds eye;

Combination Melchizedek Method & Tuning Forks
Sept 2, 2019
HURRICANE DORIAN

I was involved with a group offering of Biofield Tuning to Whales the previous year. I participated in that group and communicated with one of the Whales. In this session I decided to try working with Hurricane Dorian after it made landfall in the Bahamas. I was hopeful it was possible again with the tuning forks in combination with the Melchizedek method of energy and set the intention much the same, to communicate and help. The intention was to stand in the eye of the storm and ask permission to connect. I was successful and asked to gently send energy through with the help of my Spirit Team along with friends and colleagues to help steer it away from the Eastern Coast as it would do much harm coming to land. It feels very powerful and playful at the same time. It has a very low, powerful tone in the vibration of its voice in communicating. It replied it plays with the Wind & Oceans and was unaware it was harmful. Dorian obliged and said it did not wish to harm and would allow the help. Dorian expressed it did enjoy the energy coming through and the beautiful tones of the forks. It concluded by mentioning that no one had ever spoken before and enjoyed it. I did another that evening at 9pm est, another the following day at 1:30pm est and asked if any in the group wished to participate.

Tuning Forks

September 3 2019

HURRICANE DORIAN

Thank you all that participated, we are seeing movement away from land. As I tuned-in to Dorian, it was challenging for it to move quickly, because of its immense size. Dorian also relayed to me the Whales and Dolphins were enjoying the energy coming from all. It assured me it was still working to move away from land. I offered one more follow-up evening of sending energy at 9pm once again to help Dorian, if any in the group wished to jump in. My personal offerings were from 1 hour to 1½ hours each.

Yin and Yang

The left and right sides of the human body are yin and yang energy, being male and female. All humans have both energies within. In this process of biofield tuning, a practitioner uses an unweighted fork in the biofield or aura around the body on both sides, yin and yang energy. A practitioner can locate distortion frequencies in specific timelines. This energy of yin and yang comes from our parents as we grow. Feminine energy is on the left and masculine energy on the right. If our parents are wounded, emotionally or physically, we only receive what they have available, some being ancestral. Our parents came through with their own lessons to learn and experience. If they are depleted in some way, we in turn will have some depletion until we are able to work on the self, bringing balance to the whole. A practitioner starts at the five-foot edge of biofield or aura away from the body. This is the birth line, where the journey begins. Our bodies don't recognize their own noise being out of sync until we introduce a tuning fork. We are simply combing through this field of energy toward the physical body from the free edge toward each of the chakra centers. We are removing distorted energy by smoothing, lifting, and integrating it back to one's own unique frequency, bringing it back to entrainment.

Right Side Is Masculine, Yang Energy

Temple: Reflecting on the past

Throat: Speaking but not being heard

Heart: Emotional caretaker and overdoing (saying yes but meaning no)

Solar Plexus: Anger

Sacral: Guilt and shame

Root: Busy-ness, overdoing, and overthinking

Knee: Challenges moving forward, confusion, and obstacles. The knee can also be self-sabotage that prevents new things from coming into play.

Foot: Next steps, where we're going, and how we feel about it. The foot is also grounding or physical injury.

Left Side Is Feminine, Yin Energy

Temple: Thinking and worrying about the future

Throat: Not speaking up, or not speaking your truth or being shy or overbearing guidance

Heart: Sadness, grief, loss, and depression

Solar Plexus: Self-esteem, self-worth, and powerlessness

Sacral: Rejection and disappointment

Root: Things one wants to be doing but does not

Knee: Holding onto things and challenges with attachments

Foot: One's grounding may be off, causing footing in life to be off. The foot can also represent being stuck, wanting to move away from a stressor but being unable to do so. Also, grounding may be off or there may be a physical injury.

CHAPTER 14

The Melchizedek Method

After working with the Reiki energy vibration for years, I realized it opened the door to bring through many higher frequencies of healing. Melchizedek energy lineage is what I was called to move forward with. The Light Beings of the Melchizedek frequencies lower their vibration and embrace us wherever we are on our personal journey. The Melchizedek energy is similar to Reiki, but it taps into the fifth-dimension vibration of understanding, universal divine knowledge. This method of energy balancing uses a whole new formula for clearing and balancing. This work is very old and was taught to Jesus by his teacher Melchizedek when he was offering his healings to the masses. This method of energy balancing is much older than Reiki and uses a different formula for clearing and balancing than Reiki, with sacred geometry. The Melchizedek method is much more than a light body activation of a healing and rejuvenation technique. It's a whole new formula for body health, harmony, and spiritual ascension. The techniques in this method are unique and unlike any other. This method uses a particular sequence called the KL formula (meaning kadmon light formula). Kadmon is another name for light body.

This works with the four elements: earth, fire, water, and air.

It also works with the four light body groups: 1) the lower eight bodies of earth, the chakra base; 2) the cosmic eight bodies of fire;

3) the divine eight bodies of water; and 4) the God-illuminated eight bodies of air.

The kadmon light body field is made up of thirty-three layers, each having a color and vibration attached to it. So whichever sequence is needed by the person or group healing, this comes through to help the body repair. It removes old paradigms, balances, and heals itself on a much deeper level. And for those who have trouble pronouncing this name Melchizedek, it is pronounced mel-keys-adeck. This field of energy within and around us is the kadmon light body or hologram. As we continue, each group is represented by color and vibration frequencies and is organized by the Angelic Realm, including archangels, angels, ascended masters, and light beings. Chakra energy centers run up and down the front and back of the spine. They are cylindrical and cone shaped and are like an open vortex of spinning energy! The front centers are known as the giving centers, sending energy out to others. The back centers are known as the receiving centers, receiving energy for the self. That's where the balance comes between giving and receiving! We need to maintain balance in these centers.

Merkabah

We use sacred geometry using a mer-ka-bah and an om-ka-bah. These are the flower of life holograms. They depict how all life comes from a singular source, which is represented by the circle in the middle of the pattern. As we move along in this work and upgrade in vibration, the direction or flow of energy changes. The mer-ka-bah we bring in flows to the left, and the om-ka-bah flows to the right. We also work with the pineal gland in this method. It's the only gland in the body that's not connected to the nervous system and responds only to frequency signal and light. It's kind of ironic that I'm involved in this particular healing modality and sound-balancing instruments because they do complement each other! And this particular modality wasn't something I went looking for. It found me!

The pineal gland is very small and is the shape of a small pine cone. It points toward the center of the brain. As one awakens and opens up to spiritual awareness, the pineal gland begins to turn in an upward position, and intuitive abilities and more begin to fully open. The eye of Horus is an Egyptian term. It symbolizes the pineal gland. There are Egyptian and Pleiadean ties to this. When we are calcified by using fluoride, chlorine, and more, we are unable to connect as readily to divine universal source. The eye of Horus rests in the center of the brain and is called the pineal gland. It is the doorway to the higher realms and actually looks like an eye. This cumulative healing works with the individual to transform life from the inside out. This healing work uses sacred geometry going deeper into the human body. Clearing the unconscious mind that creates lack, fear, and discomfort dissolves at exactly the pace one can comfortably handle. The energy body is cleared of confusion and heaviness with these high frequencies. It awakens wisdom and the love frequency within, reconnecting with divine source. As the imprint of old wounds and destructive patterns comes to the surface of consciousness, they gently dissolve and leave, creating more space in conscious awareness. This multidimensional healing process clears a person's energy bodies, chakras, and meridians and restores the body's original divine blueprint (DNA), drawing energies of divine source and the earth. Together the highest frequency of love is used to heal the human physical and etheric spiritual bodies, returning them to a state of health, wellness, and receptivity for healing rejuvenation. This empowered state of conscious awareness, which is our ultimate goal, can only be truly reached through awareness. These frequencies and methods lead us toward the deep inner relationship that is vital to knowing self, to living in authentic power. As we let go of what doesn't work, we access more of what does and bring more of our true, clear, divine self into embodiment, uncovering our natural gifts, talents, and purpose.

CHAPTER 15

The Emotion Code with Magnets

This elegant work I've only just begun to use since the turn of the year is about finding and releasing trapped emotion with magnets. We use a chart with two columns of emotions each totaling thirty per column and one row displaying each organ. Trapped emotions are usually under the skin's surface and are invulnerable to magnetic releasing. As a practitioner goes through the process of identifying the emotion, it comes to the surface of the physical body, coming to consciousness. This process is invisible, but the location of the trapped emotion can be determined through muscle testing. When it is found, the test will show as weak. When the emotion comes to the surface of the body, it is now vulnerable to being released magnetically. This is released with three rolls of a magnet. Once an emotion is released, it'll be processed by the body. There is a healing period, usually one to three days. (Symptoms may be similar to the detoxing one goes through with biofield tuning.) It's rare that people experience this, but we can't predict who will.

The Heart

A magneto cardiogram measures the heart energy field. The heart's energy field is twelve feet in diameter (the holographic field). Feelings of love or affection for another will show the heartbeat in another's brainwaves. Transplant recipients get the affinities, memories, and loves of the donor.

The electrocardiogram was invented in 1895. It measures the heart waves and the heartbeat. There's a new machine called the magneto cardiogram. It doesn't measure the electrical part of the heart but the magnetic field of the heart. When hooked up to the heart, it measures the heart as being about twelve feet in diameter. They've also found that when we are feeling love or affection for another person, suddenly those heart waves show up in the body of the other person in their brainwaves. We're actually sending them something invisible when we feel love or affection for them! The heart is the core of the human being. Divine source doesn't look at the outward appearance. It looks at the heart. What does that really mean? The heart is the core, the seat of the soul. It is the seat of all creativity, of who we really are. This is where a heart wall comes in.

We have two brains. The brain in the head doesn't feel; the brain in the heart does. So when we have a wall around the heart brain, it's isolated. We become capable of doing things that we would otherwise not be capable of. It's like when we see someone in the news doing something terrible to another person. Let's talk briefly about inherited emotions. There is a difference between trapped emotion and inherited emotion, which is received from a parent at conception. Like we receive DNA from Mom and Dad, we receive inherited emotion the same way. This may go back several generations. It's important to find out exact genealogy of the emotion (a mother's, father's, grandfather's, etc.) This is released with ten rolls of a magnet. This is different from a prenatal emotion. Prenatal almost always show up in the third trimester of pregnancy. We don't know why this happens, but this is what is seen. Very rarely are they outside of that range. Absorbing prenatal emotion is most always from the mother, but it can be from the father. (Almost all of the time it's from the mother.) Inherited emotion is usually discovered when the practitioner is taken to a certain column or row on the chart, and the emotion is undeterminable! At the point we use the word *inherited* while administering muscle testing to discover the emotion.

CHAPTER 16

Chakras

Here is a brief synopsis on each of the chakra centers and how they work. When an experience arises that creates a reaction within you, ask yourself how you are feeling. This will help you locate the chakra that is out of balance and needs healing.

The chakras are energy vortices that pull energy in from our environment and also send out energy. They are cylindrical and cone shaped. The front chakras are the giving centers (energy we give to the world), and the back chakras are the receiving centers (energy we receive for the self). If we are having difficulties with our chakras, we will have difficulty in our lives. Our chakras will literally pull events, situations, and/or people to us like magnets who have the same kind of chakra distortions working within them, so we can learn from each other. Like attracts like, and we reflect distorted chakras and energies back and forth to each other. Likewise, opposites attract as well if you have a somewhat balanced chakra system, meaning your kundalini has risen and you have activated the light within you, which means you are a lightworker/healer. People who have very distorted chakras may be both attracted and repelled by you. Those who are attracted to you are sincere and desire to heal. They understand that sometimes uncomfortable and dramatic experiences may be felt in the presence of a lightworker and the clearing they're going through. However, for those who do not wish to heal, which means they are not ready to accept responsibility for their lives as yet, they will absolutely detest being in your presence and may even respond to you in a very negative, energetically explosive way because you are bringing things up in them they are not ready to deal with. However, for the most part we attract situations and events in our lives that reflect back to us, including our own issues and distortions within our own chakra system. If your kundalini has been awakened, has risen to the crown, then you may have two areas you need to discern: attraction because it is your own lesson or perhaps you are assisting others with their lessons and healing.

A Breakdown of Each Chakra

Root Chakra: This is the chakra that brings out feelings of fear, lack of trust, and not wanting to be here anymore. When these feelings arise, we withdraw our spirit from the body, becoming ungrounded, leaving us feeling spacey or in a dreamlike state (the ethers), trying to escape physicality. This can become an issue if we don't slow down, breathe, and meditate. It's helpful to use some type of sound instrument in meditation in the beginning to help quiet the white noise/chatter in our minds, whether with a CD or live tuning forks, crystal singing bowls, Tibetan bowls, or having one to play. Just spend ten minutes a day at the end of the day and you'll notice a positive change. If left unattended, they can bring on scattered energy, losing focus in the moment, and being overreactive, which can even create more karma for ourselves. Also, it can leave us vulnerable and susceptible to likeminded and hence angry situations or people. We can assist this chakra by getting in touch with the physical body through exercise and healthy habits. Focus your energy on people, places, and things that nurture, creating a sense of safety and well-being. Fear-filled events or movies, fearful spiritual/religious beliefs and interactions, etc., will keep our root chakra out of balance.

Sacral: This can cause us to feel overly emotional, confused, secretive, and disconnected from others and encourage ust o be overindulgent in areas of life such as with food, sex, drugs, alcohol, shopping, etc. We also may feel antisexual and shut down our beautiful life force/sexual energies, leading to depression. The sacral feelings all point to repressed emotions that need to be brought to the surface to be healed and released; we do this by feeling these emotions. Allow the self to go there.

Journaling and feeling the emotions will help dissolve the shadow of the secrets/things we don't want to deal with so we can gain more light.

Solar Plexus: This can cause us to feel controlling, manipulative, angry, the need to always be busy (which is an escape from dealing with our inner stuff), competitive, and the need to be right. This chakra can go in the other direction as well, leaves us feeling powerless, weak, passive, and low energy. We can help heal this chakra by accepting responsibility for ourselves, by taking back our self-power, and by allowing others to think and be who they are, focusing on the self. We also need to heal our inner anger. We have been told anger is bad, so we store it. Find a healthy way to release angry energy in the energy field, without hurting another. Otherwise we attract angry people to us, igniting that anger within. This is a prompt for us to heal it.

Heart Chakra: We need to manifest love for our self, so the love we're able to give to others is real. Feeling unloved and unlovable, we cannot truly give to others what we have not already created for ourselves. If we are feeling betrayed, depressed, critical, and jealous and feel we are not deserving of self-nurturing or self-love, this is a prompt this chakra is out of balance. When we forgive ourselves of any faults, past or present, we are able to naturally forgive others because we realize we are each here learning difficult lessons, oftentimes through difficult situations. Forgiveness is a huge lesson of the heart chakra, but so is setting healthy boundaries out of self-love with those who are stuck in the chaos and drama of life. Sometimes we may need to forgive and love from a distance du to self-love and self-preservation. Our energy and vibrational frequency are our responsibility. Use your heart to discern your feelings. What feels light and right for you may not be for another. That's okay!

Throat Chakra: We cannot speak our truth if we are feeling we are not heard. Speaking with words of love is key! If all our other chakras are out of balance, we may be speaking with the energy of fear, emotional imbalance, and anger. No one will want to listen when this kind of energy is being projected. We need to learn how to speak in a balanced, grounded, thoughtful, loving manner. For us to have our throat chakra needs met, we need to learn how to speak and how to listen so people will hear. We need to be aware of the vibrational frequency we are emitting with the power of our voice. Convenient silence serves no one, especially our own energy field.

Third Eye Chakra: This causes feelings of no imagination and feeling disconnected from reality, like we are not validated, are disconnected/detached from our higher guidance, and unable to see things from a higher perspective. Meditation releases fear in a healthy way, tuning into our inner wisdom, and will help us heal this chakra.

Crown Chakra: This can cause us to feel confused, disconnected, nervous, insensitive, uninspired, and disconnected from the earth and divine source. Meditation and healing the lower chakras helps us to open the crown chakra, which will help us feel more connected, loving, and compassionate with others. Meditation will also help us balance the central nervous system and open us up to our higher guidance.

CHAPTER 17

Orbs

What are these beautiful balls and beams of light? I personally have only viewed these particular colors below and captured some on camera. This is the information I received on their meaning from spirit team.

- Red orbs represent vibrance and stability.
- Yellow/orange orbs represent movement.
- White orbs represent purity.

This image was my first experience with orbs, but I didn't know it at the time. It was a random photograph taken during the summer of 2008 at Ossipee Lake, New Hampshire, at my cousin's campsite. I had just finished giving a Reiki treatment to one of his friends who had some back pain. After the treatment, having some fun, I started randomly taking pictures of people at the campsite. This beam is what showed up. The universe is showing us that healing energy is all around us if we choose to learn and tap into its knowledge. Look closely—you can faintly see the side profile of my cousin's face in the background.

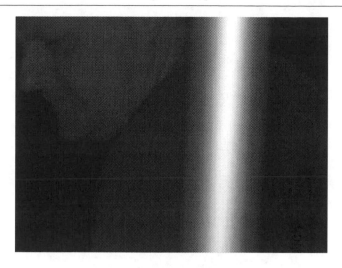

Cousin in background after a Reiki session, an Orb beam showed up next to him while at his campsite

An orb in my living room after playing crystal singing bowls

Orb at the Melchizedek Certification Ceremony, 2012

Orb after a Sound Bath at a yoga studio in New Hampshire

Looks like it's snowing in my Living room, 2015

Meditation/Spirit Team
Orbs
August 7, 2017

They are pure energy, the essence of divine energy. Angels are high-vibration energy. They need no material form.

Q: So it's the angelic realm coming through then, is that correct?

A: That is correct. They are here to help. Sometimes they can be seen, if they slow their vibration enough.

Q: So when you say they are here to help, how are they helping?

A: Their vibration helps those in need around them

CHAPTER 18

HEB

Spirit Team Coming Through
January 22, 2018
On Highly Evolved Beings (HEBs)

Q: I'm asking for your help to learn more.

A: There are highly evolved beings with you who have been with you for some time. They wish to communicate with you.

They are from outside your galaxy, not from your dimension. They are not Pleiadean, Arcturian, or gray alien. They are highly evolved beings. They are very curious and anxious to speak with you. You are on the right path. They will speak to you soon.

Q: Well, you have my attention. Why not speak to me now?

A: They are with you at this moment and would enjoy conversing.

Q: Why would they enjoy conversing with me? Why me?

A: They find you interesting and are curious about your strength.

Q: What does that mean, strength?

A: Your will, your determination.

Q: Well it's much like my father's was or like his personality.

A: No, there is more there than he had.

Q: What is it that's so curious to them?

A: They find it all interesting, and you in particular because of your simplicity of life.

Q: Simplicity in what way?

A: You keep things simple and have a colorful character.

Q: Is that supposed to be a compliment?

A: You have a happy, upbeat personality and are loving, caring, and optimistic. Need we say more?

Q: Only if you wish

A: Well at this time we'd like you to consider something.

Q: Okay, what is that?

A: Your vibration is much higher than you realize.

Q: Okay.

A: Why have you not considered doing more things with your energy?

Q: Good question. I think in my early life, fear was a big factor. All of this awareness we as a race seem to be coming into was not openly available when I was becoming introduced to this. And now ... well, I know my vibration, but I'm not sure really where I should, could, or would take it. I'm aware of only a few.

A: Well we are here to help you open that door to your God-given abilities. We are here to unlock what holds you back. You have much more ability than you give yourself availability to use.

Q: I don't really know how to expand it out or in what direction

A: You have our attention now.

Q: LOL! Okay, now what?

A: The next time you meditate in the morning, ask us for direction.

Q: What about right now? We're here together.

A: You need to be in an altered state.

Q: So being in alpha state is enough of an altered state?

A: It is.

Q: Why do I need to be in an altered state?

A: We need your attention.

Q: Anything further you wish to pass along to me at this time, divine source, about the HEB we are speaking with at this moment?

A: They have much they wish to teach you.

Q: Give me a for instance.

A: They wish to teach you how to better use your energies for the common good.

Q: No specifics?

A: Well, talk to us. What do you feel deep inside? What we're asking is to concentrate on you. What do you feel?

Q: Okay, here we go then. Here are a few things that piqued my interest long ago: the movie Resurrection, the book Know Your Magnetic Field by William E. Grey, and the episode "Empath" of Star Trek that I watched as a child.

A: Well okay, we can help you tap into these, all of them if you like or just a few.

We are here to help. We look forward to speaking and working with you. Love to you.

CHAPTER 19

Food

This chapter gives a little insight into how I take care of the body with organic eating. Below is a list of foods that are alkaline and acidic. I am a vegetarian, but I must admit I do eat fish. And this was not something that happened overnight! This took many years for me to get the hang of. I stopped eating dairy products, breads (except for occasionally Ezekiel), meats, and processed foods. I start my day with a smoothie. My diet consists of tons of vegetables, including broccoli, cauliflower, peppers, mushrooms, spinach, kale, tri-color quinoa, beans of all types, onions—well, you get the idea. In my smoothie I add ice cubes, raw spinach, hemp powder, vegetable protein powder, blackberries, blueberries, strawberries, cinnamon, oregano, half of a banana, and a heaping tablespoon of peanut butter. It starts my day and I'm not hungry until about two o'clock in the afternoon. I eat my largest meal of the day then. That usually consists of some fish, chopped cucumbers, onions, celery, and tiny tomatoes with balsamic vinaigrette dressing and either tri-colored quinoa or a yummy bean salad. The bean salad consists of three types of beans, chopped onions, celery, one teaspoon of relish, several green olives dices, and dairy-free mayonnaise. Yummy! And for dinner, I have something light, like Ezekiel bread with leftover bean salad and a small cup of chocolate humus for dessert. (The lunch and dinner menus are contingent upon the season.) Now I know this *dessert may not sound appealing, but I use one heaping tablespoon of chocolate humus, cashew milk to thin, and one teaspoon of chunky peanut butter. (I don't drink dairy milk because it contains carrageenan, a red seaweed that's cancer causing.) This is yummy. Don't knock it till you try it! And my drink of choice is water. So there you go—a little insight about my own eating. Let's get into some of the foods that are good for the system. The human body is built to naturally maintain a healthy balance of acidity and alkalinity. The lungs and kidneys play a key role in this process. The value below can vary slightly in either direction. The pH value ranges from zero to fourteen.*

- *Acidic: 0.0–6.9*
- *Neutral: 7.0*
- *Alkaline (or neutral): 7.1–14.0*

Alkaline Foods

Avocado, broccoli, almond, spinach, celery, cauliflower, asparagus, beetroot, cucumbers, kale, apples, mushrooms, alfalfa, snow peas, brussels sprouts

Acidic Foods

Grain, tomato, grapefruit, pineapple, apples, walnuts, grapes, oat, blueberry, pomegranate, fish cabbage, collard, maize, sugar, dairy products, peanut, oranges, meat, pistachio nut, deli meats, white rice, caffeinated drinks, chocolate, alcohol, mint, tomato, onion, and garlic.

These healthy foods as well honey, blackberries, strawberries, raspberries, and blueberries are very acidic.

What to Eat on an Alkaline Diet

Eating less acidic and more alkaline food helps reduce the backflow of acid into your esophagus. These foods include: many vegetables such as spinach, fenugreek, okra, cucumber, beetroot, carrot, broccoli, cabbage, coriander, cauliflower, sweet potato, eggplant, onion, peas, pumpkin, and radish and whole foods, like vegetables, root crops, fruits, nuts, seeds, spices, whole grains, and beans (especially lentils).

Drink alkalize beverages, such as spring water and ginger root or green tea or water with the juice of a whole lemon or lime.

How Do You Reduce Acidity in the Body?

Eat green vegetables, fruits, roots, and nuts. These are alkaline and keep you away from acidic gases. Vegetables should be the focus of meals, not meats. Reduce the intake of acidic food like eggs, refined sugar, meat, white flour, and dairy.

Alkaline Levels in Fruits That Help the Body

Low: Coconuts

Medium: Raisins, grapes, blueberries, oranges, apples, cherries, apricots, grapefruit, avocado olives, green banana, pears/peaches lemons

High: Blackberries, nectarines, strawberries, persimmon, raspberries, tangerines, limes, papaya, pineapple, watermelon, cantaloupe/honeydew

Alkaline Levels in Vegetables That Help the Body

Low: Snow peas, carrots, cucumbers, brussels sprouts, cauliflowers, mushrooms

Medium: Artichokes, eggplant, beets, okra, peppers, summer squash, baked potato, zucchini, broccoli, cabbage, stringbeans without formed beans

High: Asparagus, onions, celery, collard greens, parsnips, mustard greens, kale, winter squash, sweet potatoes/yams

Some of the Benefits of Alkaline Eating

Too much acid decreases the supply of oxygen. It decreases the cell's ability to repair and collect nutrients and fights against fatigue.

Teas: Most teas are mildly acidic, but some tests show certain teas may be as low as three.

Herbal Teas That Are Alkaline

Herbal teas are derived from the leaves, roots, flowers, and other parts of plants and include chamomile tea, green tea, alfalfa tea, and red clover tea.

Coffee: Drinks like alcohol, coffee, and even some carbonated water are also said to promote acid formation in your body. Organic produce is often recommended because the soil is said to be richer in alkaline-forming compounds.

Seasonings That Are Alkaline

Spices such as cinnamon, curry powder, ginger, mustard, and chili pepper are among the most alkaline.

Herbs That Are Alkaline

Dandelion root, garlic, burdock, turmeric

In Short Acidic, Neutral, and Alkaline Foods

Acidic: Meat, poultry, fish, dairy, eggs, grains, and alcohol
Neutral: Natural fats, starches, and sugars
Alkaline: Fruits, nuts, legumes, and vegetables

Protein

Eggs, almonds, chicken breast, lean beef, fish (all) oats, cottage cheese, Greek yogurt, milk, quinoa, lentils, kidney beans, chickpeas, pumpkin seeds, flax seeds, sunflower seeds, chia seeds, Ezekiel bread, fish, brussels sprouts, peanuts. (Broccoli is one of the healthiest vegetables, loaded with vitamin C, vitamin K, fiber, and potassium and is also believed to help protect against cancer.)

*Research shows a diet high in protein can produce excess acid and a diet high in plant foods leaves the body neutral or alkaline. So, if we eat a lot of animal protein with few vegetables, we would be slightly acidic all the time.

Meditation Spirit Council
Eating Meat
March 31, 2017

    The DNA is sorely shifted and tainted when eating meat. Meat is dense. Eating fish is much less dense; the DNA strands can handle the frequencies. While eating meat offers much in the way of protein, it taxes the nervous system and immune system.

CHAPTER 20

Random Insights during Meditation

Meditation with Dad
August 30, 2017
His Transition and What It Was Like

Q: Dad, what was it like? Was it different than you thought?

Were you surrounded by a bubble of white light, orbs of light, or beings that had some form, but minimal or something else altogether?

A: Actually in your timeline, I was asleep for many years. But here there is no time, so it was almost immediate. It was very peaceful. I had many beings around me. Once I was fully awake, there was more learning to go through. It's a little like going to school on your side, but more relaxed.

Q: Did you see a tunnel when you finally transitioned out and let go of your consciousness here?

A: No, I didn't see a tunnel. I just went to sleep and woke up with all these beautiful beings of light around me. Some are very tall, and some are not. They are white in color. They glow actually. I've learned many things since I've been here. They tell me you requested to come through this time to help. While I've been here I've been able to spend much time with you. Being with you has been remarkable. There is so much to learn, and being around you, I've learned much. The things you learn on the earth far exceed what you think you're learning. I can tell you more.

Q: I'm ready.

A: When I'm here and you're there, it's like movies and advertisement images of us blending, merging, like a hand in a hand, for instance. We are right there near you. The only thing that separates us is vibration. The frequency where you are is slower, denser, heavier. The experiences learned, though, are so incredible. You may think at times it's all dull, slow, or boring, but it's amazing how many things you can do there in physical form.

Q: It's quite remarkable this suit we wear. Some are better than others (meaning health). I love this, Dad. Being able to chat like this is peaceful. I just want to say something here. No matter where you went, all animals were very drawn to you! I always remembered that about you. Were you able to see anything before you left? Like in surgery, some can see themselves over the table or like Uncle Dickie who could meditate during work, walk the building, and remember consciously who he saw and what they were wearing. Anything like that happen for you, Dad?

A: No, I was feeling very ill and just went to sleep

Q: Anything else you want to talk about being on the other side?

A: No, I just want you to know I've enjoyed being around you and watching the things you do. You do some incredible things on a daily basis.

Q: You were just as amazing when you were here. You were going all the time, constantly doing something, running, going here, going there, fixing things, helping someone. I know we had the same vibration frequency.

A: *You are just so loved on this side. You work very hard. You help many people. There are so many things you don't realize about yourself. Your abilities far exceed what you use on a daily basis.*

Q: *Dad, are you allowed to point out or elaborate on some of these abilities?*

A: *I can if you like*

Q: *Okay, very good. Are we talking about the human race in general or me?*

A: *You.*

Spirit Team Stepping In

It gives us great pleasure to speak with you at this time.

Q: *Who's this?*

A: *Your spirit team. Divine holy spirit is with you and would like to speak with you at this time. Your father will return momentarily.*

Q: *Okay, very good. I'm here to listen and learn.*

A: *It has come to our attention you are about to step into some new shoes.*

Q: *What the heck does that mean?*

A: *You're about to step up in vibration. You're to do more than you realized you could. We'll explain. As you move forward from this day on, things will look different and will feel different as you continue on your path.*

Q: *Well in a good way or just different?*

A: *It will most likely feel odd to you. In a good way, but odd. Your vibration is different than many you have been associated with, and it will continue to grow. If you like, we will continue.*

Q: Okay, but, I'm losing the connection. Could I speak to my dad again?

A: He is still here with you. We want to tell you he appreciates your work. He has learned much from being with you.

Q: So Dad, do you have anything else?

A: I just love you. I just love you.

Q: Thank you, spirit team and Dad. I just love the support from Dad.

Aunt Jonnie Sue Coming Through (Mother's Sister)
March 12, 2018 (she was very ill the last three to four years of her life)

I am here free of pain, fit as a fiddle! I am here requesting to help work with you. You're amazing. You're doing things I never would have imagined. It is time for all of humanity to wake up. I'm so proud of you. This has been a long ride, and you are now coming into your own power. As we work together, I'll help to show you things. It's important, as your spirit team has told you, to stay connected. I will be by your side with you through time. You will be doing many more amazing things soon. You are ready to move forward, you'll see. I love you very much. I'm here for you as you know how this works. We were together many times as relatives. This one unfortunately we were too far from each other, but we were in the same vibration again together. I'm still in transition learning. Do you have a question for me?

Q: Travel for work: Sedona or North Carolina?

A: Sedona maybe, Carolina maybe. They will show you areas that resonate with you.

Q: If you could calculate in linear time, how long were you gone before coming through?

A: It was similar to your dad—several years.

I love you very much. I will speak to you again. There is only love here.

Q: I know, so I've been told. Are you on the new earth?

A: Yes, I am on the new earth. It is beautiful. It's everything you're looking for. You will be here.

Q: Anything for inspiration to bring along? Anything I should or shouldn't be doing? The pita bread I eat is organic. Is it good or bad for my system?

A: Not great, not bad.

Smoothies and frozen veggies are okay. Try raw foods, and stay with light food. I love you. I will come back. I'm not far.

Q: Thank you for coming through.

Meditation/Spirit Team
March 14, 2018

If you follow the progression, you are on track. We will help. We are not here to hinder, only to help. There are many levels to existence, and there are many dimensions and galaxies. As you progress, you can choose which you'd like to experience. Archangels and angels are very high on the ladder of progression. Divine source has many councils. There are teams of councils that work together in groups. If one does not wish to experience any longer, one can choose to stay with divine source.

Meditation/Spirit Team and Pleiadeans
July 20, 2019

We are here with the Pleiadeans. They wish to speak with you, if you are ready to move forward.

Q: Divine spirit team, if you wish, I am ready.

A: We are here with you. We are the Pleiadeans. It gives us great pleasure to come through and speak with you. We are pleased you are open to receive messages. As we move forward together, there is much information to bring through to share with humanity.

Q: I wish to say thank you for coming through to help, as I believe we are in need.

A: As we move forward, we have information about time travel or as you refer to it, astral travel. When one starts to astral travel, one may not remember once one has transitioned out, as you did as a young girl. You knew when you were about to leave but couldn't hold the vibration once you were out. We are here to help people understand this, to learn and practice.

Q: Do you have names, or are you speaking as a group?

A: We are here with you as a group.

Divine child, we are here with the Pleiadeans. They wish to express their gratitude for allowing them to come through to speak with you. As we continue now, one subject we'd like to touch base with you on is the astral travel. This is something many will need information on. Meditation will be key to slow down and listen. Mainly in the beginning one must slow down. It gives us great pleasure to speak with you.

Q: Thank you. You as well.

It will be important for people to stay hydrated. The food eaten must be clean to start this journey. Eat organic, non-GMO foods, and it is important to stay away from sugar and meat. This food is too heavy, and it will not allow the vibration of the system to receive. Once a person has been following this for a time and meditating, it will become easy. Once they are in a regular routine, they will be able to remember where they have travelled and who they have seen and spoken with. The astral travel is contingent on one's readiness. In meditation it slows the mind down to relax and receive.

Q: What are the benefits of astral travel?

A: This is a very good question. It helps the conscious mind expand and awaken to the subconscious mind. Once the two can maintain a balance, they will learn much. This is the next step in the evolution of humankind—to be able to do with ease daily, not as a hobby. This is where humanity is going to bring them into the fifth-dimension frequency. Energy balancing is crucial in helping and supporting the system to move along to the higher frequency.

There's more. Are you ready?

Q: I am.

A: You will see a good many changes as you continue to follow this. Now as one begins this, it's a slow process. There is no quick shortcut. One must practice clean eating, hydration, and exercise of some kind (movement), along with the meditation and energy balancing. While we are here with you, we have more to discuss with you. Because of the new work you are involved in, the emotion code, you will see great changes come. The life you lead now will change. As you turn the corner, you will see why there are delays. We'll change the topic for a moment and talk about the energy work you do. It has helped many. It gave most the spark they needed to help themselves. Not everyone will gravitate to this work. The newest energy work you're involved in now, emotion code, is very powerful. The Melchizedek, tuning forks, and emotion code will be the modalities you do the most work with. It'll just be the need. Follow your heart. You are on the right path. We will conclude at this time. We will return again soon.

Meditation/Spirit Team
July 26, 2019
The Chi

It's important to note that the energy moving through the body is what sustains it. It is connected to the physical body. There is no disconnect. As one goes about one's business daily, it is because of the energy moving through, the chi. This is the life support that sustains. It nourishes all cells, organs, tissue, muscles, etc. When you complete your life cycle in physical form, you die a physical death because the chi leaves the body. This life force chi is the universal connection to the divine. This field of energy around the body can become very heavy with static build up. You are like radio receivers. If one maintains a daily meditation and include an energy modality in one's life that resonates, it keeps the body organs and field of energy around the body clear and in harmony with universal source. Keeping one's vibration as free as possible from undue static, helps maintain harmony in the body and to universal divine source.

CHAPTER 21

Testimonials

Emotion Code

I was fortunate today to be visited by Sherryl. I had been having a constant pain in my chest. I thought I was having a heart attack. She determined the pain was from another area of my body and was able to release the pain with her magnet technique. The pain has completely gone away and has not returned for several months. I will no longer refer to her as just Sherryl but instead as the Amazing Sherryl. Thank you, Amazing Sherryl!

—Kim J., 2019

I had a second visit on October 20, 2019, with the Amazing Sherryl. I had eye surgery several months ago, which did not go well. I have been experiencing eye pain. She released thirteen trapped emotions from my system today. I will follow up with an update after I have had time to process all of this! Thank you again!

—Kim J., 2019

My husband and I have been friends of Sherryl and her family for many years. I would hear about the work Sherryl was doing through her mom and was always intrigued by the science of energy work. Recently Sherryl and her mom visited our home in Maine on a lovely Sunday *afternoon. In our conversation we talked about some physical issues that I had experienced. Sherryl introduced the emotion code using magnets to my husband, Kim, and me and performed a session on both of us that proved to be healing and relieved the feelings of stress that were weighing upon my chest for some time. That evening proved to be very relaxing, and to date the feeling on my chest has not returned. Sherryl is a very bright, high-spirited, energetic soul and very dedicated to the energy work that has helped many. Thank you, Sherryl, and it was a beautiful day visiting with you.*

Dot J., July 2019

Emotional Code: Sherryl worked with me do an emotional code technique with magnets. On the way home afterward, things would often come to me that I did not realize before. That was beneficial.

—S. Bernier, 2019

Tuning Forks: Good afternoon, Sherryl. I just wanted to say you are a blessing in my life. I feel amazing today. My distant session with the tuning forks has given me more energy than I have had in a long time. It's nice to be back! I will not wait as long between sessions! Thank you again. You are an angel, and I'm glad to call you a friend of mine.

—L. Hare, 2018

General Healing: Sherryl is an amazing practitioner in the healing arts community! She is diversely trained and incorporates her studies into every treatment. Her offerings are very unique and reasonably priced. That makes it easy to find what works for you! Sherry is someone you feel you've known forever, even the very first day you meet! I highly recommend her services! Enjoy!

—Tod Dale

Tuning Forks: Sherry, I was just thinking about you. After the last time I saw you, we had another embryo transfer, and I am pregnant! I was thinking about you because I wanted to tell you that you helped me so much and we are so happy! We are having a baby! I hope you are doing well. I will forever be grateful for your services with the tuning forks in helping me open up and getting me centered. You really did help me open up and see things positively and to help me release my negative energy. So far I have been having a really stress-free and comfortable pregnancy. Thank you so much! I will keep in touch.

—L. Fontaine 2018

Melchizedek Method: I had a powerful experience from the Melchizedek healing method. Following the session, I felt renewed, clear, and reconnected to the divine love within my own heart. I have also found that I am connecting to nature and Mother Earth in new and profound ways. I would highly recommend a session!

—M. Mariner

General Healing: I've watched quite a number of videos on YouTube, and while everyone's work is great, yours was the one that stood out ... because you not only explain everything clearly, but you also use visuals (which makes it so much easier to follow, rather than just hearing someone speak on a subject). I'll be looking out for your future videos on the different chakras, etc. The background where you do the recordings is very appealing too. It's easy on the eyes and makes a person want to watch the whole video rather than click on something else. It's a pleasure talking with you and learning more each time you email. I especially like that you reply so soon. I send an email and know you'll do your best to write back soon. It's very stress-free!

—RR, New Zealand, 2018

Tuning Forks: Hi, everyone. I watched Christopher Witecki's recent interview with Sherryl on his show and tell program about her biofield tuning services. Just wanted to say that after I saw the interview, I was intrigued and booked an appointment for this past Monday. I was surprised by the effects. Initially, I did feel some of the detox symptoms, but those subsided quickly and I feel great. I wanted to mention it here as I was amazed by the experience and the fact that I could feel the results, even with the session being done remotely.

—K. Brown, 2017

Sound Bath: Upon entering I met a past acquaintance, Sherryl Comeau, who gave me a brochure and explained the powerful energizing effects that a crystal bowl meditation could provide. Needless to say, I have been hooked ever since. Following a session, my mood is lifted, my energy soars, my mind is clearer, and small nuisances no longer exist. It is a wonderful, relaxing, and powerfully revitalizing experience to give yourself. I would recommend it to anyone who is looking to lift his or her personal vibration to the highest capacity.

—E. Leavitt

Tuning Forks: In gratitude for your work, Sherry. After just two sessions at your office and one remote session, I am calmer and more coherent than I can remember ... the work continues! I believe anyone doing self-improvement work in a supporting, mindful environment can have positive results from biofield tuning therapy. Healing and resolving low-vibration, negative subconscious beliefs and biofield tuning therapy are the necessary bridges to cross on this journey creating a new life. Cheers!

—Dennis, 2018

Mediumship Clearing: I never knew there was such an adventure to experience. I found Sherryl's site purely by accident, but for a reason! Feeling out of place, lost, and confused (not sure what to expect, or if this would help), I made the call for a clearing. From the moment I spoke to Sherryl, to months later when she called just to check in, I felt at ease and found a new friend. The actual experience was life altering in a positive way for me during the session and continued long after. It gave me tools to go forward on my own until I could see her again. My two boys, thirteen and fifteen, who did not even accompany me, sent me a message while home one hour away, telling me they felt something weird was happening at home while I was personally working with Sherryl. I have recommended Sherryl to every person I know and will hopefully return soon. A very pleasant atmosphere, she was professional but more than that, friendly and personal. Everything was tailored to me. One thing I need to say is to keep an open mind. I personally felt another presence in the room with my eyes closed, knowing Sherryl was the only physical person in there with me. Sherryl allowed me to feel calm and accepting. Thank you.

—M. Lord

General Healing: I was referred to Sherryl by a friend, and I am so glad I phoned her. She did remote healing on me, and I found the experience beyond wonderful. I highly recommend it to everyone. Thank you, Sherryl.

—*T. Hermann*

Human Tuning Fork: I have found great benefits and healing through Sherryl's work. She truly is the human tuning fork because she tunes right into you, holding space and with the energy happening around you. Both in person and remotely, Sherryl does an excellent job. I enjoy and thank her for her work.

—*N. Tomassinni*

Tuning fork sessions with Sherry are the most powerful healing experiences I have had in my life. For my first session, I hoped to clear a blockage in my relationship with my twenty-four-year-old daughter. We had a good relationship but sometimes strained. Just a few days after the tuning forks session with Sherry, my daughter remarked to me that she was sorry for the grief she had caused me and that she was grateful for all that I do for her. Wow! The blocks and karma just melted away. In my second session with Sherry, I intended to clear blockages in my career and life purpose. I knew from the previous session that I would have to schedule the session on a day I had off work because the sessions are intense and my body must detox for a day. It is an amazing experience. Just a few days after that session, my mind and attitude about my career and life purpose just made a profound shift. Nothing external happened, but my perspective shifted and allowed me to see that I am already successful and am on my path.

A sense of peace about my career now has allowed me to enjoy each day and observe the blessings. I am truly amazed that remote tuning fork healing is so intense and so profound.

—Angela, Denver, Colorado, February 2018

EPILOGUE

As we come to the close of this book together, it's time to move along to the next chapter in our lives—what's next. I will return with another book as I continue my own journey of searching and educating myself as well as others in the healing arts. I believe life is a series of continuous life lessons and learning on a soul level, not simply the ego level. And don't misunderstand—the ego is important. We as a species on this plane of existence are the only ones with this. We were given free will to learn to distinguish for ourselves distinctions of character and more. It's a person's sense of self or self-importance, our personal identity, but can also be self-conceit. Through my experiences of love, happiness, joy, sadness, grief, and loneliness, I've started to recognize profoundly positive transitions. The trials and tribulations have taught me to be more patient. Accept people for who they allow us to see, through the armor we all wear to protect ourselves. (The armor is simply fear of something.) We never know just what their journey has been. In the end, I believe all experiences/lessons are designed to help us evolve. My favorite saying is, "We're a work in progress."

Last, for those of you who have gone through ethical and moral responsibilities of one's parents struggling with dementia, I commend and applaud you! The reason I bring this subject to light is that I too am in the midst of this with my beloved mother and best friend. Since the unexpected passing of my beloved father three years ago (in 2016) and Mother's sister one year ago, she has slipped into dementia. My thoughts on this are that while they travel between the two dimensions of 3D and 5D, just love them, be with them as much as possible, and love them. When they are here, they long to be on the other side, to stay with divine source, where there is no pain or confusion, only love and beauty.

I will leave you with one example I experienced firsthand in July 2019. One day about two o'clock in the morning, Mother came to my room and woke me, asking, "Where is Dick?" (Dick was her husband and my father.)

I replied, "He's not here."

She replied, "Whose house is this?"

I was completely taken by surprise, as this had not happened before. I walked her back to her room and lay with her (as I do each night until she falls asleep), reassuring her Dick was all right and she would be also. I reassured her that he watches over her and is always by her side. That seemed to help calm her as she slowly fell back to sleep. I later did a meditation and asked my father to come through (as he has done on so many occasions) and help me understand what happened.

I asked, "Did she return too fast and became disoriented?"

His reply was, "No, it's not that she came through too fast. She didn't want to leave this time."

I live with Mother and care for her full time. I still work out of my office two days a week for those who prefer in-person work rather than remote. I also continue with remote energy sessions both locally and across the country outside of those days. Since I am her guardian, she is once again taking organic supplements daily with the help and guidance of my friend and colleague Dr. Tony Lebro, a medical intuitive I work with, out of his wellness center, A Lebro Center for Well Being. His center carries the organic supplements I order for Mother through

Standard Process and Gaia. I have successfully removed her from all but one prescription drug. During her temporary stay at assisted living, they refused to administer it to her. She has improved tenfold because of the supplements and continued energy healing. My being with her through this is as much a blessing for myself as it is for her. I've learned much more about myself than I ever would have with my day-to-day living and learning. Practice meditation daily, eat lighter foods, and stay away from sugar and caffeine as much as possible. Exercise the body, be outside in nature, stay hydrated, and drink more water to flush out the system.

Message from Spirit Team

Divine child of God, this is a very interesting point and one that should be included in the book. It is important to note that, when one has been diagnosed with dementia, one is very close to the other side. Many can hear and see the other side on a conscious level. As we continue, most coming through now have requested this. There are extraneous circumstances they are not able to handle and elect to go out this way. There are cycles to complete.

Another Message from Spirit Team

As you know, your mother visits with your father often now. She has been with him on many occasions. Their love for each other transcends time. They have been together many times. The love they feel for each other is strong. When it's time for her to leave, she will leave peacefully.

Your mother and father are calling each other. They will see each other again, dear heart. As we close, we will speak to you again soon.

***

I conclude now with the hope that you find this book to be helpful and educating. Continue on your spiritual journey, and stay open and mindful of your surroundings, nature in particular. Be open to new concepts and discoveries, and bring your own spirit team with you. There will be many adventures and experiences for you on your own spiritual voyage. Remain steady and true to yourself. Till next time ...

Stay tuned, and stay connected.

—Sherryl

RECOMMENDED AUTHORS

Dr R. Tony LeBro, medical intuitive
www.alebrocenter.com
Enjoy the Benefits Without the Risk for Optimal Health

Dr Bradley Nelson
www.discoverhealing.com
The Emotion Code/The Body Code

Eileen McKusick, sound therapist
www.biofieldtuning.com
Tuning the Human Biofield

Neale Donald Walsch
www.nealedonaldwalsch.com
Communication with God

Sol Luckman
www.crowrising.com
Potentiate Your DNA: A Practical Guide to Healing

Susan J. Ackerman, astrologer
www.lifeinsightastrology.com
The Gift of Inner Peace

Delores Cannon, Three Waves of Volunteers
www.delorescannon.com
Delores Cannon has extensive information on wave volunteers.

Ruth Montgomery *(crossed over in June 2001)*

She was a nationally syndicated news columnist in the '40s until her retirement in 1969. She worked with a spirit team giving information on what happens after death and wrote two books with the help of psychic medium Arthur Ford, who crossed over in 1971.

ABOUT THE BOOK

In this book, "A Change in Perception" Sherryl with her Spirit Team shares with you her personal experiences connecting with her Team of friends and relatives that have crossed over, Angels and Light Beings. Writing with warmth, clarity and a mix of humor, she brings understanding by helping to educate people through some of her own experiences. Her goal is to help as she shares her practical, but spiritual guidance. Sherryl believes Meditation exercises daily on this journey, can help anyone get in touch with their own Divine Spirit Team, Guides, Angels, Light Beings. She believes each of us, with the help of our Team and a healthy balance of Energy Work, can replace doubt with trust and understanding. This book is about opening the mind to possibilities beyond what's directly in front of us. To find peace through change, to work "with" life, not fight against it, to awaken one's belief. That it's ok to think outside the box and believe we "can" accomplish our dream. The knowledge is already within…
www.energyworkstudio.com

Printed in the United States
By Bookmasters